LOVE ME LIKE YOU MEAN IT

poems by

Lesléa Newman

For Fern and Faith

For Wendy,
with all
good wishes,
Lesléa Newman
11/90
PS Long distance
relationships
are HARD!

Acknowledgements

I'd like to thank all my teachers, especially Allen Ginsberg, who taught me the importance of breathing; Anne Waldman, Pat Donegan, Margaret Robison, Joan Larkin and Irena Klepfisz, who were, and are, wonderful role models of vibrant women poets; and Tom Lux, who told me I was doing not only myself, but the whole world a great disservice by not taking my writing seriously enough. I am grateful to Betty Kopit, Arachne Rachel, Felice Rhiannon, Linda Dearstyne, Judy Sloane, Sarah Van Arsdale and Marilyn Silberglied-Stewart for believing in me and my work over the years. Thank you to Julie Hannah Brower for her editing help, and Jane Philomen Cleland for her photographic expertise and for being my big friend. A very special thank you to Irene Reti for creating HerBooks, and for making *Love Me Like You Mean It* part of that vision. And lastly, as always, I am very grateful to H.P. and all her loving gifts.

Typesetting by TypaGraphix, Santa Cruz. Printed in the United States of America by McNaughton & Gunn.

ISBN: 0-939821-28-1

Some of these poems have appeared in the following publications: *Common Lives/Lesbian Lives, Dark Horse, Earth First, Gay Community News, Heresies, Hungry Poets' Cookbook, Poetessa, Sinister Wisdom, Sojourner, Spirited Women 1988, Suicide Notes, The Sun, Touching the Fire.* "One Spring" appeared as the frontispiece for the novel, *Good Enough To Eat* (Firebrand Books, Ithaca, NY, 1986).

"Love after love after love after and finally" was a runner up in the American Poetry Association's 1987 love poem competition, and was first published in Volume VII, Number 4 of the *American Poetry Anthology.*

"Train to Poughkeepsie" was first published in *Long Shot* journal.

CONTENTS

PART FOUR: *And I Was The Sky*

PART FIVE: *All Your Favorite Songs at Once*

PART SIX: *A Chain to Wrap Around the Earth*

Nothing but a Miracle

Part I

Legacy

I.

Two came from Russia
and two came from Hungary
arriving in New York
all four strangers.
Two of them met in a deli in Brooklyn
and two of them met in a place forever buried
        on their lips underground.
Each two met and married and bore three children
like the six tips of a Jewish star
        pointing towards eternity.
One of the three
met one of the three
in a high school in Brooklyn
met and married and bore three children as well,
one of whom grew up
to arrive on this snowy morning of her thirtieth year
strong, beautiful, and me.

II.

I look at my life:
these hands those feet
this face that belly
all mine.
This table those chairs
these plants those pots
that rug this bed
somehow we have all arrived.

I look at my life:
some days are calm as a glass of water
        high on an empty shelf
some days are stormy as a raging ocean
        crashing against the sandy shore
some days I have left behind
some days I have left

I look at my life:
it is nothing
but a miracle
these sheets those shoes
this head that hair
this heart
it is no accident
I am here

III.

Grandma, how old were you when you came here?
I don't remember.
Do you remember the boat ride? Do you remember
    Ellis Island?
What's there to remember? I'm an old lady,
    it's not so important. Eat some soup.
But Grandma, I want to know something about
    your life. Tell me a story.
Tell? What's there to tell? I'm an old lady.
Some days my feet hurt bad, some days my feet hurt
not so bad. You want some chicken? Here, take this piece,
it's not so dry. Listen, I'll tell you one thing.
The most important thing is your health. You have your health,
you have everything. And I'll tell you one more thing.
The worst thing is to be alone. Some days I talk to the walls
just to have someone to talk to. Some nights I'm afraid
to fall asleep, I should wake up dead and no one would know.
Believe me thirty years is a long time to be alone.
Maybe I should have married again, but who would think
I should live so long? You finished the chicken,
good *Mamela,* have some applesauce. You're such a good girl
shayna maideleh, oy you should only get married
and live a long happy life.

IV.

Lesléa Newman
daughter of Florence Newman
daughter of Ruth Levin

3

daughter of Fannie Zuckerman
daughter of

Fanny Zuckerman
mother of Ruth Levin
mother of Florence Newman
mother of Lesléa Newman
mother of

Where I have come from is where I will go

Now I am the mother
of my own life
I have created it
I have nurtured it
I have held it in my hand
I have let it go
May my mother
and her mother
and her mother
and all the mothers before that
who carried me in their wombs
a tiny secret, a treasure
a joy, a hope, a dream
may they all be proud of who I am
and what I have done

For I am the last daughter
and my life is a precious stone
a cut and carved and polished jewel
that will brighten the world
for an instant
like a pair of *Shabbos* candles
whose flames reflect
in a kitchen window
in a *Kiddish* cup
in somebody's dark eyes
before fading, flickering
and finally surrendering
to the night

Shabbos

I arrive at your door with a bag
full of *challah,* candles, candlesticks,
apples, honey, a bouquet of irises,
a *Klezmer* album, a cookbook
from the Jericho Jewish Center,
each recipe calling for two packets
of sweet 'n' low or one can
of Campbell's cream of mushroom soup.
"*Shabbos* to go," I announce
as you take the bag from my hands.
We light the candles and bless
the bread and wine, stumbling
over the transliterated prayers.
After dinner I tell you it is a *mitzvah*
to make love on the *Shabbos.*
Your eyes grow big and worried.
"What's a *mitzvah?*" you ask.

Oh my sweet, my Sabbath bride,
if only our grandmothers could see
us now: born a few years apart
in neighboring towns
yours from Vilna, mine from Minsk,
each fleeing pogroms to arrive
on strange soil
yours to Denver, mine to New York,
each to have children who
would in turn have only daughters,
daughters who many years later would find
each other in the foreign land
of Western Massachusetts,
find each other and grow
to love each other as fiercely
and as passionately as their grandmothers'
will for survival.

One Day in the Middle of the Night

One day in the middle of the night
you find yourself back in your childhood
which was, for the most part, happy.
You are in the park with your best friend
Meggy. She pumps her legs up and down
as the swing set groans and creaks
until her feet kick the sky. You sit
below her, legs spread, scratching
your name in the dirt with a pointed stick.
The big boys are at a safe distance
across the park, playing with balls
and mitts. Dusk falls. Your mother
calls through the screen door, tucking
back a stray strand of hair with her hand.
You run home. The whole house smells
like something wonderful to eat.
Other mothers call.
Children scatter

and suddenly you are awake, unsure
for a moment of where you are.
Then you see, it is she, your lover
lying next to you in the blue darkness,
her head pillowed on your arm. She turns
to you, unable to see your tears
but sensing your sadness. You feel her
concern as she holds you and you fold
yourself into the crook of her arm.
For how can you explain that the beauty
of her caring fills you
with an immense grief and longing
for each day you have spent together
is one day less you have left
and that child sprawled happily in the mud
is gone forever and will never know
the woman she grew up to be
weeping in her lover's arms.

Brighton Beach, 1959

On summer nights after the sand and sea-salt
were scrubbed out of every inch of me
I'd lie on the couch in a baby blue nightie,
feet tucked under
wet hair streaming down my back,
listening to my mother
frying something in the kitchen
and my father singing in the shower
as the rest of the world disappeared
into the descending darkness
that surrounded us all safely
as the blanket tucked up to my chin
when I'd lie in my bed with a full belly
lulled by the murmur of grownup voices
rising and falling like waves
while I dreamed of floating on my back
in the steel blue space between ocean and sky

From a Childhood

When my nipples were two small snaps
sewn onto my chest
and my hair fell down my back

in one long braid,
when my armpits were bald
as kneecaps, before the blood

ran down my legs month
after month after month,
I lay awake in bed listening

to my father's footsteps
fading down the hallway
like a freight train disappearing

around a bend,
leaving me alone
in the warm blue darkness

thinking about death:
lying still and perfect
as a stone, my mother

my father, all my friends
walking by, their tears falling
onto my polished face

as they bend to kiss me,
the closing of the coffin lid,
the clumps of dirt falling

like rain, then nothing
nothing
nothing but my body beginning

to stiffen, unable to move my hands
my feet, unable to open my eyes
I lay in my bed really terrified now

the night pressing down on me
heavily like the lead shield
at the dentist's office

that always makes me sleepy,
only to be brought back to life again
by the sound of my mother's laughter,

the clink of the Mah Jongg tiles,
and the scraping back of someone's chair
as she rises to fill the coffee cups

My Father's Body

Across the kitchen table
I watch my father's hands
put things into his mouth:
crusts of rye bread dipped in *shmaltz*
pieces of Wonderbread soaked in gravy
gobs of cottage cheese
gulps of orange juice
whole boxes of raisins
with sun maidens on the cover

My father's hands are square
his knuckles swollen from years of cracking.
There is a big callus on the middle finger
of his right hand from years of writing.
He doodles columns of figures while he eats;
his 2's look like v's
like little birds flying off the page

My father wears cotton boxer shorts
with paisley designs like paramecia.
He puts his feet up on the coffee table
and his arm around the back of the couch.
When my mother goes upstairs
he pulls me close to him
and smokes a fat cigar
as the TV blares

His eyes are green
his hair is black and white
his teeth are yellow
his breath smells like instant coffee and spit
his neck is scrawny like a chicken
his chest is full of wiry gray hair
his belly is round moving up and down
his legs are skinny
his knees are bony
his feet are small and dry

He has one gray hair sticking out of his left nostril

He has a big brown mole on the outside of his right elbow

His lips are soft
his cheeks are bristly
his fingernails are painted clear like a girl's
his teeth are filled with real silver and gold

He is six feet tall and weighs 186 pounds
I know my father's body
better than I know my own

It

The first time I told anybody
about it
it being my piano teacher
my piano teacher being
Mr. Schwartz
Mr. Schwartz being the one
who put his hand
where it didn't belong
where it didn't belong
being under my butt
my butt being
on the piano bench
the piano bench being
under his hand
his hand being
under my butt
my butt being
a part of me
me being Lesléa
Lesléa being a ten year old girl
it shouldn't have happened to
it being what
I told you about
you being the one
with tears in your eyes
your eyes being
the ones
the first ones
that ever really looked
at me
me being Lesléa
Lesléa being the one
it shouldn't have happened to
every Wednesday at 3:15
it being my piano teacher
my piano teacher being
Mr. Schwartz

Child's Sestina

He's in a bad mood, my brother mouths
to me as he leaves the room, closing
the door. First he makes
me play scales, my fingers fumbling on the dark
keys. He places his big hairy hands
over mine, his arms around me from behind

to show me how to do it right. I'm behind
in my practicing, his mouth
frowns in disapproval. He hands
me my music book and sits close
to me, pointing at the dark
notes which make

no sense to me, yet he makes
me play them anyway, a pencil tucked behind
his ear, poking out through his dark
hair. The gum in his mouth
smells stale. I wish he would close
his lips or put his hand

over them or something. His hands
are huge and pale. They make
me nervous the way he opens and closes
his fingers, the way he puts them under my behind.
I clamp my mouth
shut wishing it would get dark

and the lesson would be over. His dark
eyes stare at my hands
stare at my mouth.
Sometimes he makes
me kiss him behind
the door — why is it always closed

and where is my mother? Why does he sit so close
to me on the dark
piano bench? Why does my behind
feel so funny on top of his hands?

Will someone make
him stop kissing my mouth

He's too close   his hands
are touching my   dark place   making
my behind hurt   please take his mouth away

My Father's Lap

I am 16 years old and I am sitting on my father's lap. I am 16 years old and I am sitting on my father's lap. I am wearing an orange sweater dress with a white stripe around the collar and a white stripe around each sleeve. My father says this dress makes me look sexy. I hate this dress. I am sitting on his lap and we are in the living room with Uncle Seymour, Uncle Harvey and Uncle Alex. I hate this dress and their voices drift past my ears heavy and slow like the smoke from my father's cigar. I am 16 years old and I am sitting on my father's lap. 16 years old sitting on my father's lap. I keep my back stiff and my feet on the floor. My father pets my hair from the top of my head down my shoulders down my back down my waist down to his lap. My hair is thick and curly and black. I will set it tonight on rollers the size of orange juice cans when everyone leaves. When everyone leaves. My father's hand is heavy at the back of my neck where it rests for a minute, heavy as my uncles' voices, heavy as the smoke from his cigar. I am 16 years old and I am sitting on my father's lap. 16 years old on my father's lap. He kisses the top of my head and plays with my fingers as he holds my hand. He plays with my fingers as he holds my hand and his big college ring rubs against my pinky. It hurts. It hurts but I do not move. I do not move because I am a ghost. I am a ghost and my father is a ghost and my uncles all are ghosts. The TV is not a ghost. The TV is on and it is not a ghost and I hear a football game. Every now and then a loud cheer bellows out from the screen and every now and then a loud burst of laughter erupts from the kitchen. From the kitchen where my mother and Aunt Rose, Aunt Ethel and Aunt Miriam are making lunch. I am 16 years old and I am sitting on my father's lap. 16 years on my father's lap. My mother and my aunts are taking little cookies filled with chocolate and jam out of a white cardboard box and putting them onto a plate and laughing. Little cookies filled with chocolate and jam and laughing. My mother won't let me eat any because I am getting too fat. I am getting too fat but later when everyone leaves I will eat them all. When everyone leaves I will eat them all until nothing is left. Until nothing is left and nothing remains. I am 16 years old and I am my father's lap. I am sitting on his lap and he is petting me like a dog and my dog is sitting at my feet waiting to be petted but I cannot pet him because my father is petting

15

me. My dog's back is stiff my back is stiff the back of the chair is stiff I am drowning in all this stiffness and my father's hand is heavy at the back of my neck where it rests for a minute, pulling me down. I am drowning and my father can't hear me and my mother can't hear me and the ghosts can't hear me. No one can hear me because I say nothing. Nothing is said nothing is heard nothing is left and nothing remains. I am 16 years old and I am sitting on my father's lap. I am 16 years old and I am not sitting on my father's lap. I am not sitting on his lap because everyone has left and nothing is left and it is time for bed. It is time for bed and my mother and my father are in their bed and I am in bed and my dog is in my bed curled behind my knees and the nightlight is on. I am 16 years old and the nightlight is on because I am afraid. I am afraid of the dark I am afraid of the ghosts I am afraid of the shape of my clothes piled high on the chair. I am afraid to fall asleep because I am afraid I will never wake up. I will never wake up and then I will be a ghost I don't want to be a ghost I am afraid of the ghosts I am afraid to fall asleep. I am 16 years old and I am afraid to fall asleep so I pet my dog. I pet my dog from the top of his head to the tip of his tail. I pet my dog the way my father pets me. Sometimes my dog whimpers in his sleep and sometimes I wish I was a dog but I am not a dog I am 16 years old and I am afraid to fall asleep. I am afraid to fall asleep until I think about my father. I think about my father dying and that makes me cry and then I feel better and then I fall asleep. I think about my father dying and that makes me feel better and then I feel better and then I fall asleep.

Making the Earth Tremble

Part II

One Spring

The air was thick with the promise
of lilacs and rain that evening
and the clouds hovered about my shoulders
like the mink stole in my mother's closet
I tried on from time to time.
I was sixteen and I knew it.
I tossed my head like a proud pony
my hair rippling down my back in one black wave
as I walked down the sultry street
my bare feet barely touching the ground
past the sounds of a television,
a dog barking
a mother calling her child,
my body slicing through the heavy air
like a sailboat gliding on lazy water.

When the blue car slowed alongside me
I took no notice
until two faces leaned out the open window.
"Nice tits you got there, honey."
"Hey sweetheart, shine those headlights over here."
"Wanna go for a ride?"
I stopped,
dazed as a fish thrust out of water
into sunlight so bright it burns my eyes.
I turn and walk away fast
head down, arms folded,
feet slapping the ground.
I hear, "Nice ass too"
then laughter
the screech of tires
silence.

All at once I am ashamed of my new breasts
round as May apples,
I want to slice them off with a knife
sharp as a guillotine,
All at once I am mortified by my widening hips,
I want to pare them down with a vegetable peeler

until they are slim and boyish.
All at once I want to yank out my hair by the roots
like persistent weeds that must not grow wild.
But I am a sensible girl.
I do none of these things.
Instead I go home, watch TV with my parents,
brush my teeth and braid my hair for the night.
And the next day I skip breakfast,
eat an apple for lunch
and buy a calorie counter,
vowing to get thinner and thinner
until I am so slim I can slip
through the cracks in the sidewalk
and disappear. And I do.

Appetites

I.

I raise my arms
as she lifts the cloth
brushing my face
her hands are soft
feeding me something sweet
stroking my cheeks my hair
singing a little song
only the two of us share
as she tucks me in
the blankets pulled up
under my chin
she lies with me
until I fall asleep
dreaming
that this is how it was

II.

I sit at the kitchen table
staring at my oatmeal.
She won't let me get up
until I finish it
and I hate it
even more than I hate her.
I hear the water running
as she moves back and forth
carrying glasses and dishes
from table to sink
and I swing my legs back and forth
wishing I was outside somewhere
instead of sitting in this stupid chair.
She sponges off the table
sweeping crumbs into her hand
finally saying I can go
if I just take one bite.
I pick up a speck of oatmeal
with the edge of my spoon
close my eyes

hold my nose
open my mouth
swallow
and throw up all over the place
crying as she screams,
"Next time I'm going to mop it up
with your hair. Now get upstairs."
I climb the steps slowly
wishing she would die
down there on the kitchen floor
with a green bath towel
full of vomit in her hands

III.
Late at night I sneak downstairs
moving through the darkness
as though I were underwater.
I open the refrigerator
and the bright light blares
like an alarm clock.
Quietly I take out
2 pieces of Wonderbread
2 pieces of American cheese
2 Devil Dogs
2 Good Humor bars
and a bagel.
I sit down
and the plastic chair beneath me
squeaks.
I eat
the soft foods
becoming part of my soft skin.
When I am done I rise
my belly round and full
as I climb the stairs
tip-toeing past my parents' room,
remembering my mother told me
she hasn't had a good night's sleep
since her first child was born.

I imagine her lying there
next to my father,
one eye open
like a whitefish behind the Deli counter,
its lidless eye forever staring,
its body rigid on the ice,
waiting patiently for the stranger
who will peel back its skin
and pick apart its bones
to devour the sweet meat underneath.

IV.

At the restaurant my mother falls
upon the rolls. "Thank God! I was starving,"
she says, her mouth full of dough.
She bites into a hamburger,
her long red nails digging into the soft bun
and shoves french fries
and onion rings into her mouth
while I push around
my tossed salad and sip diet soda.
After the plates are cleared away
she orders cheesecake
asking the waitress to bring her
two packets of Sweet 'n' Low,
one for her coffee and one for her purse.
When we get home we each migrate
toward our own bedrooms
like homing pigeons lighting
on branches for the night.
Before I fall asleep
I run my hands along my body
feeling my collarbones, sharp as swords,
my belly curving inward like an empty boat,
my hipbones jutting out like rocks
along a jagged shore.
I sleep like a baby
in a cradle
in a hammock

in a spoon being lifted
toward a pair of red lips
two rows of yellow teeth
and a tongue curled like a finger
beckoning me to enter
the thick warm darkness behind it.

V.

Mama
I never called you Mama
though I always wanted to.
Mama, will you tell me you love me?
Will you tell me you think I'm strong
and beautiful?
All I remember was you telling me
to lose weight
do something with my hair
and put on a brassiere.
Mama, tell me you're proud of me
for living on my own
because that's what you taught me
the whole time you shlepped us kids
to dance classes and Hebrew school,
whenever you made supper and did the dishes,
each time you picked up Papa's suits from the cleaners
and his socks from the floor
the creases between your eyebrows were saying:
I don't want to be doing this.
The little lines that pulled
at the sides of your mouth were saying:
I can't stand this.
And the sighs that escaped your lips
everytime you stubbed out a cigarette were saying:
only a fool would settle for this.
Mama, don't you see I listened to you?
For once in my life, I'll admit
you were right.
Mama, come sit at my table
and tell me stories
about when I was a little girl,

how I was born with thick black hair
long enough for a ponytail,
how the nurses all took turns combing it
and how you cried
because you were so happy I was a girl.
Mama tell me about you and Papa,
how he'd lie on the floor
with his hands under his head
his eyes closed
while you played the piano
and Grandma fried blintzes in the kitchen.
Mama I am hungry
for these stories
of how we all loved each other.
I want to hear them again and again
so I can pretend
I remember

Supper

I look at my mother
across the kitchen table,
behind the wooden salad bowl,
beyond a dozen dinner rolls.
Smoke rises from either side of her;
a Chesterfield smoldering to her left,
a cup of Instant Maxwell House steaming
to her right. Through an empty
family size bottle of Coke,
I watch her place forkfuls through
frosted lips and my eyes trace the food
down, into her round full belly
pushing against the table.
And I think
I lived in there once
eating her food
breathing her air
talking all I could
even then

Hunger

Inside me
the hunger inside
the hunger inside
the hunger forever
like those funny wooden dolls from Russia
the hunger inside
the hunger inside
me forever
is demanding
to be fed

In the middle of the night
I wake to feed it
eating and eating until my belly
is stretched tight as the skin
on an ancient drum

Still I hear the cries
of mountain lions perched on my hipbones
small black bears clinging to the tree of my spine
angelfish swimming in schools through my veins

And I eat more and more
until my thighs grow fat and get in each other's way
as I walk down the street, like two women
in the A&P trying to squeeze by each other
their arms full of canned peaches
and hamburger rolls

And still the construction men
and the garbage men and the businessmen
wink and whistle and yell "Hi Beautiful!"
as I pass looking for more food to give this body
that can no longer be contained by skirts or slacks
or sweaters and certainly not by me
and why couldn't they see

that the hunger inside me
is churning like a volcano

threatening to devour me
unless I keep eating and eating

and like a child's pet iguana
that will grow big enough to fit its cage
I grow big as the world
making the earth tremble as I walk
leveling buildings with each step I take
everyone running this way and that
trying to get out from under my great black shadow
but there is nowhere to go

and still I feel hungry

Song for Ten Scallops

Who were waiting
in a Chinese fish market
to be scooped up, weighed
and wrapped in wax paper,
to be carried home, unwrapped
and sautéed with soft mushrooms
and beads of brown rice,
to be slid into a wooden bowl,
sprinkled with tamari
and lifted with chopsticks,
to be chewed, swallowed and digested
to become part of my body
to become part of the earth.

Ode to My Hips

Look out boy
these hips are coming through!
These hips'll knock you off your feet
if you don't make room for them to move.
These hips sway
these hips sashay
these ain't no size 3½ slim Brooke Shields
teenage boy hypocritical hips —
these hips are woman hips!
These hips are wide
these hips hypnotize
these hips fill a skirt
the way the wind fills a sail.
These hips have *chutzpah*
they think they can change the whole world!
When I take these hips out
for a walk on the street
and the sun is shining
and my bones are gleaming
I place my hands on these two hips
and let them speak the truth.

Train Ride to Poughkeepsie

I'm sitting in the no smoking car
and the guy across the aisle
is giving me the eye
even though his girlfriend is asleep
on his shoulder
but I'm more interested in
the want ads of the Village Voice
wondering whether I want to be

an administrative assistant,
bookkeeper, cashier, cook, dish
washer, girl friday, live in
babysitter, messenger, proofreader,
receptionist, secretary, telephone
operator, typist or waitress
when I look up from the newsprint

and see the grey Hudson rippling by
through the grey window
under the grey sky
and there's a black iron bridge out there
and some ducks bobbing up and down
and some trees
and it all looks like some black and white
foreign film I starred in a long time ago

but now this train is wracking
my body back and forth
like some half crazy mother
who's trying to cook
clean the house
wash the clothes
feed the cat and
care for the kids all at the same time

and those soft mountains out there
aren't doing me a bit of good
because it's cold in here
and the seat is hard

and I want a lover with a shoulder
to fall asleep on
while they give someone else
across the aisle the eye

Adjustments

I. *Shifting Piles*

I place a pile of credits to my left
and a pile of debits to my right.
After I type the numbers from the debits
onto the credits
I pile the debits on top of the credits.
Then I pull the carbons from the credits
and separate the copies into piles.
I interfile the piles
and bring them over to the files
where I file the piles and pull the files
making a new file of piles.
Then I make files
for the pile that had no files
and put them into a new file pile.
I take the new file pile
down the aisle
over to the table where Mabel
makes labels for April to staple.
I take the new labeled stapled file pile
back down the aisle over to the file
to be interfiled with the pile of filed files.
After I file April's piles
I get new debits from Debby
and new credits from Kerry.
I carry Kerry's credits and Debby's debits
back to my desk
and place a pile of credits to my left
and a pile of debits to my right.
After I type the numbers from the debits
onto the credits
it's 10:00
and we have exactly fifteen minutes
to go down to the cafeteria
and drink coffee
or go out into the parking lot
and scream.

II. *Coffee Break*

Here comes the cake.
Will you look at that?
It's beautiful.
I don't know how he does it.
If you ever need a cake just ask Bob.
I had to carry it in for him you know
because of his wheelchair and all
you know and I had to hold it like this
because it was frozen you know
and God forbid I should fall.
Who brought in the cake yesterday?
The skinny one. You know, Alice.
Was that you Alice? You rat.
I can't help it. My landlord
gave it to me and I hate cake.
If I don't bring it in here it'll go bad
and I'll have to give it to my dog.
Listen to her. She gives it to her dog.
In my house it wouldn't last five minutes.
And she puts it right in front of me you know
I'm sitting there typing and I can smell the chocolate.
It's a good thing it wasn't mocha.
If it was mocha I would've slugged her.
I put the tea box in front of it and the coffee jar
so I wouldn't see it.
If it was mocha forget it. There goes my forty pounds.
You lost forty pounds? Really? How'd you do it?
Weight Watchers.
Really? Do you have to measure all your food out and everything?
No, not anymore. You get used to it, your eye you know.
I fill up on unlimited vegetables like mushrooms
and broccoli, you know? I can sit and eat a whole head
of lettuce in one night and not gain an ounce.
That's terrific.
You didn't try a piece, did you Jackie?
Just a little piece.
Yeah, right, a little piece seven layers thick.
Shame on you, a former Weight Watcher.
I know, I lost 25 pounds and put back 8 already.

But what'cha gonna do?
What a dreary day.
They say it's gonna rain all weekend.
It figures.
Hey Mabel, what's today's date?
The 23rd.
You know today I've been here for three years?
No kidding. It seems like you just started.
Time sure flies when you're having fun, right girls?
That's what I like about her, she's always joking.
You know who she reminds me of? Lucille Ball.
Yeah, you know you're right.
Someone said the same thing just the other day.
It's not the red hair and the deep voice so much,
it's the personality. She's always laughing.
Well you know what they say girls.
It's better than crying.

III. *Ivy*

I worked here for two weeks
before I noticed the stem of ivy
that had crept in through a crack
in the wall and was growing slowly
across the carpet
up towards the African violet on my desk.
I showed it to April.
"Oh wow," she said.
"That should be on THAT'S INCREDIBLE
the TV show you know, where they have
all those interesting people on
doing all those interesting things
you know, like hanging upside down
out of an airplane or something.
You know people do the most amazing things."

IV. *Out to Lunch*

We walk past the guard
on our way out to lunch.

"Let me see your ID," he says.
I unbutton my coat to show him
the badge he gave me four hours ago.
"Oy vey, do I ache," Debby says to me.
"Last night I went to an exercise class
and I can barely move."
"What kind of exercise was it?"
"Jazzercise."
"That's what you get for exercising
those old bones," the guard says.
"Now me, I say leave those old bones alone.
Hey girls, while you're going out for lunch,
why don't you just sign out now? Just put 5:00 right here.
That way you won't have to do it later.
I believe in making life easy."

V. *Paranoia*

You know this afternoon I realized that
Kerry's hair isn't really blonde and
her makeup makes her eyes look a lot bluer
than they really are and I typed New Rock
instead of New York five times in a row
without realizing it and when Annie asked me
today's date I had to stop and think about it
for a really long time
and I didn't even see April standing right next to me
with a box of paper clips in her hand for five minutes
until she tapped me on the shoulder
and I can't even tell when the muzak's on
or the muzak's off anymore because of all the other noises
going on inside my head
and why do I always look up at the clock
at exactly ten minutes to four?
I have this funny feeling
that maybe Kerry was sent here from another planet
who's trying to take over the earth
so they cloned all these women to look like secretaries
and they're slowly dulling our minds
by making us type these numbers all day long

until our brains are about as useful as empty gas tanks
and I bet I could walk in here stark naked
or drop dead at my typewriter
and no one would even notice except maybe the janitor
who comes in once a week to empty the trash
and make the same joke, "Oh so your can's full again, huh?"
Maybe I've been reading too much science fiction lately
but can it only be a coincidence that Kerry
just happens to be the first one in here every morning
making the coffee the rest of us drink?
And oh shit I just typed $3,338.83
instead of $3,338.38
and you know Veronica who sits behind Kerry
well she has dyed blonde hair too
and she mails my time card in every week
which means I have no record of my hours
so maybe this is all a dream
and I'm never really here
or maybe the rest of my life is a dream
and I'm really always here
and maybe it's too late and I'm the last one left
who hasn't been taken over yet
and they're waiting for me to surrender
so they can use this bank as their national headquarters
or maybe they've taken over the rest of the country
already and I should call the President
because I'm the only one left with any brains whatsoever
but I'm not even sure about that.

VI. *4:55*

We shut off our typewriters
put our pencils into our pencil holders
screw the tops onto our jars of liquid paper
and glance at the clock
we place our unused envelopes
into our top left hand drawers
and our sheets of carbon paper
into our top right hand drawers
and glance at the clock

we lift our pocketbooks onto our laps
freshen our lipstick
pat our hair
and glance at the clock
we straighten our tangled rubberbands
check to see our typewriters are turned off
and glance at the clock
we inspect our fingernails
notice where the polish has chipped
and glance at the clock
we uncross our legs
and glance at the clock
we smooth our skirts
and glance at the clock

VII. *5:00*

Bye
Goodbye
Goodnight
Have a nice night
You too
Take care
Have a good night
Good night
Good night

VIII. *Ode to the Secretaries of America*

The secretaries of America are spreading out
everywhere — with their orange silk roses
in thin white vases on their desks
next to pictures of their children and grandchildren
smiling at them through oval frames
next to jars of yellow and white liquid paper
lined up like nail polish
next to ceramic mugs that say
WORLD'S GREATEST MOTHER or HAVE A NICE DAY
next to pencil holders made from orange juice cans
covered with construction paper

covered with glitter,
with their sugar free chewing gum
tucked away in their pocketbooks
tucked away in their bottom left hand drawers,
with their light blue cardigans
draped over the back of their swivel chairs
with their headphones on
listening to their bosses whispering
instructions into their ears
like some obscene phone caller —
Oh secretaries of America
I hear you walking behind me in the parking lot
your high heels clicking on the pavement
your car keys dangling from your fingers,
I see you walking through Waldbaums
with shopping lists in your hands
or waiting to buy white fish at the deli counter,
I hear you calling home on company time
to tell your teenage sons to take out the roast beef
and put it on low in the toaster oven,
I see you at Elaine Powers Figure Salon
bending at the waist,
I hear you in diners munching on cottage cheese and carrot sticks
comparing the calorie content of pink and white grapefruits
I see you trying on skirts and slacks in Orbachs and Macys
looking over your shoulders
at your behinds sighing in the mirrors —
Oh secretaries of America listen to me!
Take off your girdles and relax.
Stop wearing that lipstick,
it's made of pig fat, it's not even kosher.
And don't you know, you don't have to make the coffee?
Oh secretaries of America
get up off your chairs
and take a walk in the sun
or go home and watch soap operas
with your teenage daughters and sons.
Oh secretaries of America
we love you just as you are
with your thick ankles and untweezed eyebrows
with your soft bellies and flabby thighs.

We were born out of your bodies!
We nursed at your breasts or wanted to,
we crawled into your lap
and let you rock us to sleep,
we came to you crying with our scraped knees
and let you kiss it all better,
oh secretaries of America
come crawl into my lap,
tell me about your day,
let me massage the back of your neck
your aching shoulders, your tired feet
let me give you a goodnight kiss
before I shut the light and tuck you in,
Oh secretaries of America
take tomorrow off
it's on me
take next week off
take next month off
oh secretaries of America
just take off

Who Knows You Bone by Bone

Part III

Poem

(for Frank O'Hara)

ETHEL MERMAN HAS EXPIRED!
I was rushing home from work
trying to eat dinner
and make ten phone calls
before I had to rush out
for my self defense class
but the chicken was frozen
and everyone's line was busy
or they had their answering machines on
and my purple sweatpants were dirty
and my cat was stuck up in a tree
when suddenly I read the headlines:
ETHEL MERMAN HAS EXPIRED!
There are no trees in Manhattan
and no one had an answering machine
in the '30's.
Oh Ethel
when you opened your mouth on Broadway
they could hear you all the way to Poughkeepsie
and if I had a pair of lungs like yours
I'd forget all about self defense
and just belt everyone over the head
with a song

Waiting

She stood in the living room
waiting
with all her weight on one leg
her arms folded
her head against the window
watching the evening
bloom into blueness and blossom into blackness
with the lights
going on
in the houses
all around her
and the stars.
This was not what she was waiting for
for she was still waiting waiting for what
she did not know still she stood still waiting.
And the darkness waited with her
and the darkness waited without her
and this was a comfort to her.

She made a cup of tea
and while she still stood still waiting
she waited for the water to boil
and this was a different kind of waiting
a smaller kind of waiting
in the larger kind of waiting
just the right kind of waiting
she had been waiting for to wait
while she was still waiting
and after she had waited
for the waiting the waiting came
and she waited it out
and then the waiting was over
and the waiting for the waiting
was over and then only the waiting
was left so she waited.

and drank her tea
and held the empty cup
for its warmth

held something for her
as she waited
and the darkness waited with her
and the darkness waited without her
and this was a comfort to her
while she waited
with her hands holding the cup
and the cup holding her hands
and after a while
while she was still standing still waiting
watching the night
move into mauve and melt into morning
all the lights
went out
in the houses
all around her
and the stars.

Falling Asleep During a Storm

Outside the wind roars without ceasing
like a restless ocean bruising the shore.
Windows shake with fear in their panes,
the clock's heartbeat quickens

and the chair shifts its weight
from one leg to the other.
On the stove, beans soaking in a pot
stir in their sleep, sighing my name.

At the first crack of thunder
the ceiling threatens to shatter like a shell
of a hard boiled egg cracked with a spoon.
The telephone almost screams.

Then softly the rains begin.
I dream of lush tropical forests
and wake up pulling out strands of my hair
like long dark weeds from the newly moist earth.

The Apartment House at Night

Under an icy moon
two cats
chase each other
up and down the hall
like small infinite horses

while everyone sleeps
behind shut doors

except one woman
whose head is bowed
whose breast is lifted
by her own cupped hand
to meet her own small mouth

Morning Still Life

Sunlight streaming in
through a window
warms a chair
where the cat busies herself
one leg lifted into the air

An empty teacup still warm
on the table
next to a plate dusted with crumbs
a knife sticky with butter
a plant, leaves leaning toward the light

In the next room a woman
her elbows lifted like wings
her fingers woven into her hair
smiling at herself in the glass
the water in the bath rising

The Bath

When she lifts her hair
into a bun
it is like peeling a peach
exposing the sweet moist meat
to the night's teeth

When she slips her robe
from her shoulders
it slides down her back
smooth as a lover's tongue
landing at her feet

When she reaches into the tub
the waters part like lips
to embrace her hand which she
lifts listening to the drops
falling from her wrist

Love after Love after Love after and finally

you arrive in the arms
of your favorite chair
and drink the tea
that has been left
just for you.
At the bottom of the cup

you find the stranger
who knows you bone by bone
who has been waiting patiently
all this time
for you to discover the only one
who will always love you

Smile at your own reflection.
Gather yourself up
and be your own child
sitting on your own lap.
Rest your cheek on your own bent knee.
Forgive yourself. Live.

And I Was the Sky

Part IV

A True Story

After we made love for the first time
I fell asleep in your glorious arms
and dreamed we were making love
in the single bed of my childhood
where so much happened that only my body remembers.
Under that blue and green paisley spread
we made love for hours until our bodies were spent
and we lay quiet and content in great pools
of sweat and come. Then my father came in.
"It's raining in here. I have to close
the windows," he said, stepping past the bed
where we lay with the blankets pulled up to our chins.
Without another word he left, and you turned
to gather me in your arms and hold me delicately
against your breast just as the child in that bed
always wanted to be held after her father left
but never was. "How did that feel?" you asked,
your voice so soft and full of caring
that my heart ached to hear it.
"He doesn't have any power over me anymore,"
I answered, and then awoke to wake you too
and tell you the dream and make love again
very very gently as the room grew light.

You Love Me So Good

You love me so good
I'm not used to it
I'm used to a slap a crack
across the face   a plate
sailing through the air
in a perfect arc   slow motion
past my head through
the open window   to shatter
in pieces and pieces and pieces
six storeys below
on the street

You love me so good
I'm not used to it
I'm used to a loud angry
silence filling the room
until I can't breathe
a cold hard back turned
toward me three miles away
at the edge of the bed
lonely as an empty field
under a dark sky full
of stars too far away
to touch   no sounds
nothing   not even the howl
of a hungry old dog

You love me so good
I'm not used to it
I'm used to jagged words
ripping up the night
you asshole   you bitch
you cunt   you motherfucker
what am I supposed to do with
sweetheart   angel
honey   treasure
I can't fling those words
back in your face
I can't cringe on the couch

biting my knuckles to keep
from crying out
I can't let your words seep
into my skin and flow through
my veins like pure honey in slow
ecstacy   for more than two minutes
before I start to wonder
when you're gonna turn on me
and be someone you're not

You love me so good
I'm not used to it
yet you keep coming
around here with your cards
and flowers and especially
that hungry look in your eyes
that makes me want to kill
whatever it is
inside me that won't let you
love me unless you destroy me
the way I destroy myself

You love me so good
I'm not used to it

You Decide To Bring Her Flowers

You decide to bring her flowers even though it's
your first date and you're scared you're coming
on too strong and you don't even know if it's a
date-date or just a date but you decide to bring
her flowers even though you think maybe she just
wants a new friend though you remind yourself
she's the one who called and asked you out to
dinner but she can't really have a crush on you
can she, so you decide to take a risk and bring her
flowers because all your life you've tried to
second guess everyone else's feelings and deny your
own so you decide to bring her flowers because
anyway if you looked in the mirror you'd see
desire written all over your face as soft and
fragile as the purple petals of the iris she is now
holding with such shy pleasure in her eyes that
your stomach lurches with the wanting of her and
you decide your biggest fear is that she'll say yes

First Woman

First Woman
stood behind me
lifting a kimono to my shoulders
and I was the sky
with blue cranes gliding
to my feet

First Woman
lay above me
face full as the moon
casting shadows of light
across my breasts and belly
with her eyes

First Woman
asleep beside me
arms around my waist
like a tight silk sash
as I listen to her breath
falling all around me like snow

Small Town Sunday Morning Pantoum

We walk down the street
in search of breakfast.
We do not touch.
We are very much in love.

In search of breakfast
a dog trots up to us.
We are very much in love.
You give her a biscuit.

A dog trots up to us
happily in the sun.
You give her a biscuit
you carry just for this purpose.

Happily in the sun
people say good morning.
You carry just for this purpose
a special quiet smile.

People say good morning.
We enter the bakery.
A special quiet smile
lingers on your lips.

We enter the bakery.
The baker's glance
lingers on your lips.
He offers you a bite of muffin.

The baker's glance —
it is not unfriendly, and yet . . .
He offers you a bite of muffin
which you take, and admire.

It is not unfriendly, and yet . . .
His hand brushes my fingers
which you take and admire
as he offers the muffin to me.

His hand brushes my fingers
which were deep inside you an hour ago.
As he offers the muffin to me
I wonder what he would think about that.

Which were deep inside you an hour ago.
Now I lick them clean.
I wonder what he would think about that
and about being in a lesbian poem.

Now I lick them clean.
We buy two fresh bagels and leave.
And about being in a lesbian poem —
I can think of worse places to be.

We buy two fresh bagels and leave.
We walk down the street.
I can think of worse places to be.
We do not touch.

Writer's Block

I'm too busy
loving me
& loving you
& loving you
loving me
& loving me
loving you
to write a poem
about it
woman

so there

How We Fought

We fought with sharp pointed words
that were well aimed and seldom missed
We fought with hard stubborn jaws
and clenched fists smacking the night air
We fought over silly things
that became important
and important things that become silly
none of which I remember now
We fought naked we fought clothed
We fought about things that had happened
and things that hadn't happened
Yet we fought for each other
and we fought against each other
and we fought without understanding
Why we fought with tears and shrieks and moans
just as we had once made love
We fought and fought
until there was nothing left
and so I left with nothing
but myself

Inappropriate Emotions

On the day you meet the woman you are
to spend the rest of your life with
you do not feel particularly joyous,
elated, ecstatic. Your heart does not
leap with gladness, nor does it contract
with fear. Rather you feel a little shy,
thinking *there's a pretty woman*
as you catch sight of her
standing in the doorway
in a brown poncho
with short dark hair sticking straight up
and her head tilted to one side

You do not know
at that moment of moments
that that brown poncho will hang
over the back of your rocking chair
for many a night
that your fingers will slide through
that sea of dark hair tenderly, endlessly
that the slant of her head will become
as familiar to you as the slant of sunlight
that pours through your bedroom window
every morning
knocking at your eyes

On the day the rest of your life comes
to an end, you do not feel particularly sad,
angry, afraid. You do not weep
into your handkerchief, wailing *why me*
nor do you beg the woman for a little more
time. You kiss her goodbye and press
your cheek against her shoulder
not knowing you will never again feel
the smoothness of her skin.
Blissful in your ignorance, you start
the car, sing along with the radio
think about letters to answer, lunch

And the day after that,
the day after the rest of your life
comes to an end,
there is nothing to do
but get up, shower, dress, eat,
go to work, come home again.
It is a day much like any other
except there is an absence so present
it is clear that something is missing
and you don't feel much of anything
but bewilderment because
you now know that you never know
what anything means the moment it happens

Ex-lover

You still have me tacked up on your wall
in my favorite orange sweater
staring straight out of the photo
into your kitchen.
I've watched you
slicing carrots for juicing
and tofu for frying.
I've seen you
sitting at your little table,
a cloth napkin on your lap,
a pair of chopsticks in your hand.
I've looked on
as you've pushed your plate away
to gaze out of the open window
at the empty sky,
the same sky in the photograph,
the same sky above my head
fifty miles away.
You don't seem to understand
that besides the sky
all we have left in common
are the earth, the air
and a few painful memories.
I don't want to watch
you moving through your kitchen
or your life anymore.
I've got other things to do now.
Take me down.

All
Your
Favorite Songs at Once

Part V

After a Year of Celibacy

it sounds like something to eat
you know
cream of celibacy
deep fried celibacy
celibacy fricassee
sweet and sour celibacy on toast
everything sounds like something to eat
when you're hungry
and I am hungry
for a woman

a soft woman like a cashmere feather
a hard woman like a ball of clay
spinning between my hands
a sweet woman like a chocolate frosted
caramel covered honey coated date chopped
in half with a salted cashew inside
because a woman is like that you know
layered
like the earth
or a rose or an onion
or a chocolate birthday cake

and here I am back to food again
I'm eating enough for two or twenty
and even though I've had more than plenty
I can't get enough
of something I never wanted in the first place
and I never wanted a woman
no
I never wanted those deep dark delicious
mysterious kisses
and I'm not taking about Hershey's this time
no, I never wanted a woman

as much as I do now

Spring Fever

Oh Vicky I'm in such a state
I just can't seem to concentrate
I want to ask you for a date.
Oh God oh Goddess oh my oh dear
it's so hard being newly queer
and though I've known you for a year
I don't think that I can speak
for at least another week.
For when you call and I'm not home
you purr into my telephone
and the sound of your voice when I play back the tape
makes me feel squishy just like a grape.
I'm so glad I have an answering machine,
it gives me the shivers clear down to my spleen.
Oh Vicky
I get so sticky
wondering just how you feel
and if anything's real.
When I see you I go wild
I feel like a child
I giggle and wiggle
like a worm or a snake
I squirm and I shake,
my breath explodes in ecstasy
I pirouette in fits of glee
I write whole books of poetry
hoping that you'll notice me.
Oh Vicky dear, I really fear
I'll explode like a rocket
if I can't wear your locket.
And then there'll be little bits of Lesléa
all the way to South Korea.
And you'll gather me up piece by piece
from the cold Northwest to the hot Southeast
and patch me up as best as you can,
so what if you leave my nose in Iran?
Or my ears in Turkey or my eyes in France
oh Vicky give me half a chance,
when you dance and throw your hips around

I think that every girl in town
will soon be knocking your door down.
It's spring! The girls are all about
my heart is beating inside out.
Oh Vicky can we please go steady?
I'll even eat whole wheat spaghetti
and save some for your Great Aunt Betty
who would approve of me I'm sure
(you see I can be quite demur)
I'll pick my clothes up off the floor
I'll set my hair, I'll wear white gloves
(the lacey kind Aunt Betty loves)
I'll eat toast points, I'll drink mint tea
I'll type your resume for free
I'll even learn to water ski
if only you'll go out with me.

It's a Bitch Being Butch

Well, me and my friend decided we were too soft, ya know?
I mean cream puff and marshmallow was an understatement, dig?
We wanna be tough, see.
We wanna be so cool
you catch pneumonia just by looking at us.
So one day we go out and buy ourselves
some black muscle T-shirts and some tight jeans
and we put on our sneakers and our headbands
and our mirror sunglasses
and don't we look fine swaggering up Main Street
with our thumbs hooked into our pockets,
our keys dangling in the breeze?
Now I have to admit I felt a little naked
without my Mickey Mouse watch, feather earrings
and the cute little labyris I got at the music festival last year
but my friend says we're too cool for those kind of decorations.
So we start cruising up the street
and we decide we need new names, ya know?
So now I'm Velcro, and my friend is Venom.
We don't see any dykes to show off for
so we go get some coffee and I make sure
no one hears me order Decaf.
And as we leave the place I'm so busy being cool
I don't even notice the sliding glass door
is shut and I slam right into it
spilling Decaf all over my brand new black muscle T
and Venom starts laughing so hard
she pees in her brand new tight jeans.
Well we cut out for home then
and we pass some women sitting outside the movie theatre
laughing and carrying on some
but they sure do hush up fast
and their eyes open wide
when we turn the corner
and they start wondering
who are these new dykes in town?
And as we get closer
one of them starts to laugh
and another one says, "You look adorable,"

and I say, "Adorable? Humph!" and they laugh even more.
"I'm Velcro and this is Venom," I say,
standing with one hip thrust out
and my thumb pointing at Venom as if I was hitchhiking
down some dusty road not giving a shit
if I never get picked up.
So they all start laughing some more
except this one girl I've never seen before.
This girl is standing there in boots and a black leather jacket
with a tattoo crawling up her arm and across her chest
disappearing inside her tank top
where my eyes would sure like to follow.
Well this girl is as quiet and as cool
as a cat stalking a cockroach
and me and Venom almost choke on our gum
when someone tells us she just rode her motorcycle
here all the way from San Francisco
and suddenly Venom and me feel real tired.
We're ready to go home and go to bed.
"Do you sleep in baby doll pajamas?"
the women ask us
as we walk off
their laughter tickling the back of our necks
like a warm summer breeze.
And when we get home Venom takes off
her headband and rubs her temples
and I get into bed with my big old teddy bear
and we decide next week we'll really show them
when we get all dressed up for the big dance
in gold lamé gowns
with high heeled shoes to match.

Baby Dyke's Pantoum

Would you look at those girls
standing on the street
acting as if they own it
laughing in twos and threes

Standing on the street
in their jean jackets and Frye boots
laughing in twos and threes
cuffing each other on the shoulder

In their jean jackets and Frye boots
not saying excuse me
cuffing each other on the shoulder
when some guy bumps into them

Not saying excuse me
but watch where you're going buddy
when some guy bumps into them
with their short sharp hair

But watch where you're going buddy
some of them have tattoos
with their short sharp hair
and axes around their necks

Some of them have tattoos
my mother wouldn't like that
and axes around their necks
they don't even wear brassieres

My mother wouldn't like that
Who do they think they are anyway?
They don't even wear brassieres
or eyeliner or lipstick or nothing

Who do they think they are anyway?
How come they don't carry pocketbooks
or eyeliner or lipstick or nothing?
One of them's got purple streaks in her hair

How come they don't carry pocketbooks?
Two of them have motorcycle helmets
one of them's got purple streaks in her hair
and I think she's winking at me

Two of them have motorcycle helmets
the blonde one's name is Rattlesnake
and I think she's winking at me
you think I could learn to stand like that?

The blonde one's name is Rattlesnake
her leather pants look like they've been spray painted on
you think I could learn to stand like that?
I'd sure like to give it a try

Her leather pants look like they've been spray painted on
I wonder how she gets them up
I'd sure like to give it a try
Uh-oh looks like they're getting ready to move

I wonder how she gets them up
over her gorgeous hips and ass and thighs
Uh-oh looks like they're getting ready to move
Sure wish I could go along

Over her gorgeous hips and ass and thighs
they really are something else
Sure wish I could go along
walking all over this goddamn town

They really are something else
would you look at those girls
walking all over this goddamn town
acting as if they own it

Poem for Janie

I love Jane Philomen Cleland
because she has a million curls
all over her head
and in just as many ways

I love the big labyris that swings
between her breasts
that sway across her chest
when she dances
which is always
with her head thrown back
letting out the laugh
that starts deep in her belly
and winds up splat!
on the ceiling

I love her car Nancy the Nova
who loves my car Rhoda the Toyota
and one day they're going to get married
and have baby motorcycles
that will grow up to be Kawasakis
and we'll ride off into the sunset together
Janie Pie and I
with our two cats, Kugel and Couscous

I love it when Janie and I go to Miss Flo's
for breakfast
pretending we're cross country dykes
somewhere in Nebraska
eating home fries and whole wheat toast
and I love running around the parking lot with her
pretending we're Keystone Coppers
and I love being anywhere with Miss Janie P.C.

But most of all I love being at her house
because the walls are covered with pictures
of baby Jane squinting at the camera
and hippie Jane with long curly hair
and fierce Jane with her fingers spread like claws

and happy Jane dancing by the ocean
and sexy Jane in a Panama hat
and being with all those Janes
is like hearing all your favorite songs at once
only better
because then the real Jane comes in
smelling like hyacinths
and eating watermelon

Passover Poem

My lover is all excited. "I'll bring *Challah*
to the *Seder*," she says, pleased with herself.
I kiss the tip of her *goyishe* nose and explain.
Two nights later she arrives at sundown
with whole wheat *matzo* that tastes worse
than the box it comes in, as I mourn
for the chocolate-covered *matzo* of my childhood.
She offers to run to the co-op
for some carob-coated rice cakes.
"You're sweet," I say, "But it isn't the same."

What I really miss though
is my grandmother's chicken soup,
much better than the miso *matzo* ball
we had last year.
It's not the soup though,
it's the whole *megillah* that started
the week before *Pesach* when my grandmother arrived
from Brooklyn with all her shopping bags.
You'd think there were no stores on Long Island
the way she'd *shlep* the chicken the carrots
the onions the celery the *matzo* the *borsht*
the macaroons the *gefilte* fish the *Pasadicha* brownies
and cake mixes that tasted like wet sand.

Then came the morning of *Pesach*.
My mother, who is deathly afraid of heights
would step out of her fuzzy slippers
and onto a yellow vinyl chair.
She'd reach up into the kitchen cabinets
and hand down the special plates and cups
we used only once a year.
I in turn would hand up the *trayf*:
the forbidden poptarts, oreos, ringdings,
mallomars and Ritz crackers
we couldn't bear to throw away.
And then the cooking would begin:
such chopping and slicing and grating
and frying and *noshing* and baking

like you wouldn't believe!

It is the same today
only I do not go.
My grandmother doesn't understand.
"What, you're not coming?!" Her voice
cracks in disbelief. "I made my own *gefilte* fish —
for that alone you should come."
And she's right, I think as I hang up the phone,
for that alone I should.
But my mother, may she live and be well
and not fall off her kitchen chair
has forbidden her sons, never mind her daughter
to bring a *Shiksa* home for Passover.
And even though this woman
with the blue eyes and straight nose
tries her hardest not to confuse *Hammentaschen*
with Robatussin
this woman who eats cheeseburgers and likes
to call me *Bubbeleh* but sometimes forgets
and calls me *ruggeleh,*
even though this woman means more to me
than all the *kreplach* in Nassau County,
Tel Aviv and Brighton Beach combined,
this woman is not welcome.

So I do not go home.
But I do remember
my father sitting at the head of the table
with the Maxwell House *Haggadeh,*
his *yarmulke* standing straight up on his head
like a beanie,
I do remember opening the door for Elijah
and the dog barking to prove he had come.
I remember when we all got really hungry
we'd ask my brother to read in Hebrew
and he'd speed along skipping whole paragraphs.
I remember the year we hid the *Afikomen* under the toilet lid
and my father bribed us with real silver dollars
that had pictures of John F. Kennedy on them,
and I remember rousing choruses of *Dayenu*

with lots of mumbling in-between
because nobody knew the words.

This year I'll go to Stacy's house.
We'll sit in a circle on the floor,
have a pot luck supper
and tell stories of strong Jewish women.
Last year Grandma, I spoke about you.
"Really?" I imagine you asking,
your voice rising with pleasure.
Really.
I passed around your picture, the one
I took of you standing on the boardwalk last year
and everyone said how beautiful you are.
I told them how you came over on the boat from Russia
just you and your mother when you were ten
85 years ago.
I told them how you've lived alone for thirty years
ever since Grandpa died,
how you do all your own shopping and cooking and cleaning,
how you *shlep* your groceries up six flights of stairs
when the elevator is broken
which is more often than not,
how your house is so clean
you could eat *blintzes* off the floor,
how you don't let me lift a finger when I come visit,
how you still paint your nails red and dye your hair brown.
Everyone wished you were at our *Seder.*
Someone said I look just like you
and I felt proud.

Three years ago I came out as a lesbian
and came home
to my Jewishness.
All of a sudden Yiddish sprang from my lips
like leaves from a barren tree.
"*Gey shlufen,*" I'd murmur to my lover
as I kissed her goodnight.
"*Hock me nisht ken chayniki,*" I'd yell
at the cat who meowed to go out
two seconds after I let her in.

I developed strange cravings for *knishes,*
latkes, kasha varnishkas, bagels
and lox, chicken soup.
I hung a *mezzusah* over my door
and a six pointed star around my neck.
Last year, in the middle of chopping apples
for the *Charoseth*
I burst into tears
and nothing would console me
except listening to *Fiddler on the Roof*
weeping and singing at the top of my lungs
for hours.
I was ready to come home
but they were not ready to have me.

So this year Grandma, even though
you will be in New York
and I will be in Massachusetts,
we will both eat *matzo* and *maror,*
dip lettuce in salt water
and sit in a reclining manner,
we will both spill ten drops of Manischevitz
onto our plates and fill Elijah's cup,
we will both sing *Day-Dayenu* and say
"Next year in Jerusalem,"
we will both be surrounded by those we love
like Jews everywhere
celebrating our survival.

Because You're Not Here

Because your car broke down and the last bus just left
and the telephone is not your shoulder

Because your absence is more distracting than a piece
of apple caught in my teeth

Because my bed only has two sides when you're not in it

Because you smile in your sleep and smiled when I told you so
and the night goes on forever with or without you

Because a piebald moon is rising and you're not here
to see it or me shivering in the wooly darkness

Because you said I have hot eyes and I do
and you're not afraid of them

Because your skin is not the color of frozen chicken left out
to thaw but more like a young girl's gold earrings glinting
in the sun

Because I want to write a love poem about each one of your cells
after I count them with my tongue and thank God you don't know
anything about poetry

Because I have to travel 5,000 miles through sub-zero temperatures
to get to the light switch across the room and when I return
you warm my feet between your thighs

Because you'd rather make love than breakfast and I want to be
your toast your coffee your Spanish omelette your chestnut souffle
your crepes aux fromages avec fraises

Because you're not here now kissing each x y and z of me
and I wonder if you're sleeping eating reading a book
taking a walk somewhere breathing

Possibly

to wake and find you sitting up in bed
with your black hair and gold skin
leaning against the white wall
a perfect slant of sunlight slashed
across your chest as if God
were Rembrandt or maybe Ingmar Bergman
but luckily it's too early to go to the movies
and all the museums are closed on Tuesdays
anyway I'd rather be here with you
than in New York or possibly Amsterdam
with our eyes and lips and legs and bellies
and the sun as big as a house in the sky
and five minutes left before the world begins

A Chain to Wrap Around the Earth

Part VI

How It Isn't and Is

I want it light, playful
like the almost accidental brush
of the back of my hand against your nipple
one evening as we lie on the bed

I want it natural, unthinking:
the hardening of your nipple
against my hand

I want it automatic, spontaneous:
the way your nipple rises
to meet my mouth

I want it urgent, strong:
your hands groping and tearing
at my jeans

I want it smooth, yielding:
my wetness against your fingers

I want it uncontrolled, wild
like your moans against my ear

But this is not how it is

One of us remembers what he did to us
when we were 2 or 5 or 7
One of us remembers what she did to us
when we were 12 or 20

And one of us has to stop

Or one of us is afraid
she won't come
or she'll come too soon
or she'll come too much
or she'll take too long
or one of us has to get up in the morning
or one of us is expecting a call

So neither of us asks, offers, looks, touches
without a long complicated discussion
about how, how much, where, where not to,
when, when not to, how fast, how slow,
how hard, how soft
until half the night is over
and we wonder if it's worth it

And then I get sad that it's not easy
or at least easier
And then I get mad
that there's so much tension in our lives
and here too

And sometimes I want to kill your mother
for teaching you that passion only leads to pain

And sometimes I want to kill my father
for teaching me that love equals sex equals shame

But most of the time I kill
this desire in me
for your sweet breasts under my tongue
your warm cunt against my thigh
your hot breath in my ear
your voice rising joyous and free
from your beautiful throat
when you come to me full
of my love and your own
song

August Night

My lover reaches her hand up into me
drawing out a perfect melody
and I who never raise my voice
in anger or in song
moan and sigh, scream and shriek
from dusk 'til early dawn

Picture this:
a strong woman with lavender overalls,
short dark hair that stands up straight
and a labyris swinging from one ear
walks home from a dance;
her hands in her pockets
her steps light and firm
her body still keeping time
to the music she just heard.
Watch her undress and climb into bed
naked, the soft summer air
a caress against her sweaty skin.
See her smile as she falls
into a dream
of holding a warm girl in her arms,
their hips swaying together
their bellies whispering secrets to each other
all across the floor.

. . . My lover reaches her hand up into me
drawing out a perfect melody . . .

Now picture this:
some boys, maybe three or four
stand in silhouettes against the darkness
outside the woman's house.
Watch the tall one pour a can of gasoline
over a mattress,
down the front, up the back, over the sides.
See them all heave it against the front door
while the woman sleeps,
her cat at the foot of the bed,

her old dog's paws twitching through a dream.
Stand back as the short one lights a blue-tipped match.
Run as the mattress bursts into flames.

> . . . and I who never raise my voice
> in anger or in song
> moan and sigh, scream and shriek . . .

Now the woman wakes in terror
at the screech of her smoke alarm
against her ear. She leaps
out of bed, runs to the front door
only to be driven back by the heat
on her skin, the smoke
in her throat and eyes.
Something inside her
guides her to the back door
which opens easily
onto a calm night full of stars.
Something inside her
guides her back to the bedroom
to pull on a T-shirt
call for the cat
lead the old arthritic dog
down the three steps into the yard.
Now she stands there
wrapped in a neighbor's robe,
her arms around her dog
her house up in flames
the fire scorching
her heart.

> . . . from dusk 'til early dawn . . .

> My lover reaches her hand up into me
> drawing out a perfect melody
> and I who never raise my voice
> in anger or in song
> moan and sigh, scream and shriek
> from dusk 'til early dawn

82

Supreme Sodomy

I never thought the Supreme Court
would make it
into one of my poems
I never thought the Supreme Court
had anything to do
with my life.
I never thought the Supreme Court
would decide
I cannot kiss
my girlfriend's cunt
in the privacy of my own home.
Last night while I thought
I was minding my own business
I committed eight felonies in our bedroom.
I was arrested
by her beauty.
It was a trial
to take in so much pleasure.
But as I came and came like a tidal wave
building and building only to break
me wide open on the shores of our bed
I was afraid my moans would alert some cop
who happened to be cruising by
who now has the right
to rush up the stairs
bust open the door
throw the book at me
and haul my lover and I off to jail
for the dangerous crime
of sodomy.
Meanwhile somewhere a woman is being beaten
to death by the back of her husband's hand.
Somewhere a child is crying and bleeding
alone in the dark.
Somewhere real crimes are being committed.
Meanwhile I will consent to minding my own business
the business of loving another woman
the best that I can;
exposing my softest places

to her lips and tongue
letting her know me
letting her heal me
exploring her wettest warmest places
with my fingers and mouth
as she lets me know her
lets me heal her
and our love will make waves
across the shores of our lives
and the lives of other women,
women who nurture each other
women who say yes to each other
women who live and love together
in this crazy world
trying to survive
alive

Poem for Judith

When I moved into your sixth floor walkup
on Second Avenue
there were boxes of books, manilla envelopes
and small wooden knicknacks
all over the living room.
Your husband's things, you explained,
but he was moving out.
You were through with him,
you had a boyfriend to prove it
and I believed you.

Mornings on Second Avenue were noisy affairs.
In between the semis roaring by
and the garbage trucks backing up
loud angry words would slice my sleep.
But I rolled over,
not interested in someone else's
bad dreams
exploding
on your arms
in black and blue
welts
on your mouth
red blood

Judith
it was all so crazy.
All you had to do was change
the locks on your door. A simple act
like going to the store
for a container of milk
or sharpening a knife on a cold smooth stone.
But it would upset him, you said,
he was so fragile
he loved you so much
it would ruin his career.
You talked and talked
as more and more vodka bottles collected
under the sink

and the black and blue marks
spread across your arms
like a child's watercolor painting
of a moonless starless sky

And I couldn't do anything
because it was your apartment
and if I changed the locks
the landlord would throw me out
and where would I ever find another place
in Manhattan for $175 a month?
And so we lived the whole winter
without a window in the kitchen —
only a hole where the plate had slashed the glass
after missing your head.
I packed away my teapot and all my favorite mugs
finally realizing you were as crazy as he was
and I was as crazy as you
but what could I do
except patch up the cracks in the walls
and scatter boric acid across the floors
so nights I couldn't sleep
I'd sit in the kitchen
watching the cockroaches,
their bodies filled with poison
their homes sealed shut
their guts exploding under their hard tight shells
as I smashed them with a hammer
one by one by one by one

One day I came home to find the phone cord
clipped in two. The next day you realized
he was stealing your mail.
The day after that you signed the paper
that put him in Bellevue for six weeks.
I was cautiously relieved.
You drank less,
ironed your clothes,
sat still long enough
for the cat to climb into your lap.
One night we even had dinner together:

tortilla shells filled with meat, tomato sauce and spices
and you laughed at how much water I drank.
You showed me pictures of you
arriving in New York eight years ago:
a smiling young woman with a broad brimmed hat
pulled over one eye,
flirting with the camera.
You were proud as a little girl
displaying her very first painting
as you showed me picture after picture:
Look how thin I was
Look how thin I was

Rain fell with the twilight
my last night in New York.
As I started up the stairwell
your boyfriend ran down the steps
three at a time in nothing
but his underwear.
Your shrieks above us were punctured
with thuds steady as the footsteps
of an approaching killer
in a horror movie we've all seen
a hundred times before.
When I let the police in
they found your head a bloody mass,
your husband standing above you
his arms raised high
ready to deal you yet another blow
with the television set.
And when you came to, you sobbed,
Why did you call the police?
Why did you call the police?
I didn't answer you then
but could only marvel at the rainbow of colors
decorating your face
and the fact that you still thought
saying no to a man
would damage him beyond repair
like a fist
smashing a tooth or a skull or an eye

Holding Nina

Holding Nina
is like holding the whole universe
in my arms   for half an hour
there is peace in the world
no one's daughter is disappearing
in Argentina or South Africa
no children are staring at me
with big eyes and empty bellies
on the front page of the newspaper
no woman is being beaten by her husband
her cheekbones cracking against
his knuckles like fine china
no little girl is being forced
to touch her daddy her uncle
her big brother in unspeakable places
no nuclear missiles are holding their breath
under the ground waiting
to destroy us all

Holding Nina
helps me forget
the world is a tormented place
for half an hour   the world
is a beautiful place
where I sit with the woman I love
resting   her head on my shoulder
its gentle weight reminding me
we must not forget the goodness of the world
and all it can be
and we must not forget the horror of the world
and all it can be
so we hold each other very dear
as dearly as the world holds us
for half an hour   and then we rise
for there is much work to do

Hana's Pantoum

I am fifteen months old
I know nothing of war or bombs
My name is Hana, daughter of Khadafy
though I do not know these words

I know nothing of war or bombs
I know warm milk, pink dresses, Mama's soft cheek
though I do not know these words
I am just learning how to walk

I know warm milk, pink dresses, Mama's soft cheek
the safety of darkness pinpointed with stars
I am just learning how to walk
on my chubby legs, my feet in little white shoes

The safety of darkness pinpointed with stars
One night the whole world exploded. There was red water
on my chubby legs, my feet in little white shoes
I never learned the word for blood

One night the whole world exploded. There was red water
I wanted to make a picture with the pretty color
I never learned the word for blood
But my fingers were gone and so was my hand

I wanted to make a picture with the pretty color
Big splotches all over my dress
But my fingers were gone and so was my hand
I didn't even have time to cry

Big splotches all over my dress
I could have been a famous painter or a movie star
I didn't even have time to cry
My Mama cries all the time now, I can hear her

I could have been a famous painter or a movie star
Maybe I would have looked just like my Mama
My Mama cries all the time now, I can hear her
calling my name, remembering my dark eyes

Maybe I would have looked just like my Mama
I wish my Mama was here now
calling my name, remembering my dark eyes
that no longer see and no longer cry

I wish my Mama was here now
There's lots of little children here
that no longer see and no longer cry
Most of them aren't famous like me

There's lots of little children here
They all want someone to write a poem about them
Most of them aren't famous like me
Children from South Africa, children from Nicaragua

They all want someone to write a poem about them
Weave their names into a chain to wrap around the earth
Children from South Africa, children from Nicaragua
shattered into a million pieces like stars

Weave their names into a chain to wrap around the earth
I am fifteen months old
shattered into a million pieces like stars
My name is Hana, daughter of Khadafy

What To Write About

The way the light falls
across your face in the morning
as you move from dreams into day

The way the cat purrs
when you lift your head from the pillow
The slap of your feet against the wooden floor
How she weaves herself
in and out of your ankles
How your wrist twists as you open a can
the plop of the cat food
and the bend of your back as you place her dish on the floor

The sound each drop of water makes
against your skin in the shower
The way you pour tea into a teacup
and butter toast
The thrust of your arm into a jacket sleeve
and the way you slam the door

Your thoughts as you type letters or change diapers
serve food or clean houses
and how you feel when you have five minutes to yourself
behind the bathroom door

The way you sing off key with the radio on the way home
The lurch of the car as you shift into third
The flock of birds
that passes like a shadow overhead
and all the trees disappearing behind you

The squeak of the mailbox lid
and the letter from your next to last lover
The graceful arc of your neck
as you stand slicing vegetables
and the salad that needs something else
The way you pause
one hand on your hip
the other on the refrigerator door

The sound of fork against plate
ice cube against glass
the scraping back of your chair
the rush of water in the sink
and the flush of the toilet down the hall

The steady creak of the rocking chair
and the shadow it casts on the wall
The way the windows fill
with indigo   and then turn dark
and the stark beauty
of your own reflection in the glass
as you look up
startled by a distant clap of thunder

The occasional turning of a page like a sigh
and the cat asleep with her head on your arm

The crease between your eyebrows
and the way you bite the tip of your pen
The endless blue lines
that stretch across your notebook
page after page
like a million empty horizons
that only you can fill
with all the words
that make up your life

Love Me Like You Mean It

Love me like you mean it
like it was the very first time
that night last May
with your neighbor's TV blaring downstairs
and your dog whimpering and twitching
in her sleep
and you trembling so hard your bones
rattled against each other
and the bed squeaking on its four unsteady legs
I tell you it was like a regular symphony orchestra
in that small room
and I was making so much noise myself
it's a wonder I heard any of it

Love me like you mean it
like it was the very last time
not the next to last time
or the time before that
but the this-is-it-never-again-
not-even-one-more-time time
because some day it will be
though we probably won't know it just then
since that's the way these things usually happen —
one of us will die
or go away
or decide she needs something else
someplace else

So love me like you mean it
like this is the only time
I'll ever have to give myself
to you completely open
taking you in as far as you want to go
and then farther still
for only you can touch those places
deep inside me
where I wrote your name
a thousand years ago
in a language I had never heard
before you came home
to speak it

Secret

Sometimes
when the morning sun streams
through the kitchen window
and I'm washing the dishes
or opening a can of cat food
or sweeping potato peels and onion skins
off the linoleum floor,
I get so taken with the way
my arms move back and forth with the broom
or how pretty my fingers look
all dressed up in soap bubbles
that I just have to jump up
and dance around the house
laughing out loud

Other times
when I'm sitting in my favorite rocking chair
with the cat on my lap purring
and the clock on my wall ticking
and the evening sky a particular shade of blue
halfway between periwinkle and midnight,
I feel so content with the way
my feet push off gently against the wooden floor
and how my belly moves up and down
with each breath I take
that I just have to sigh
with the sheer delight of knowing
that everything I want
is everything I have

Photo by Jane Philomen Cleland

About the Author

Lesléa Newman was born in Brooklyn, N.Y. on November 5, 1955 (quadruple scorpio!) the daughter of working class Jewish parents, and the granddaughter of poor Jewish immigrants. She now makes her home in Northampton, Massachusetts where she writes and teaches women's writing workshops. She has worked at a variety of jobs, including secretary, daycare teacher, sales clerk, reporter, artist's model, health care worker, support group facilitator and short order cook. In the past few years she has given many readings and been a guest lecturer/teacher at schools and communities across the country, and cherishes all that she has learned from her audiences and students.

Also by Lesléa Newman:

Novels
Good Enough To Eat (Firebrand Books,
Ithaca, NY, 1986)

Poetry
Just Looking For My Shoes (Back Door Press,
Seattle, WA, 1980)

Short Stories
A Letter To Harvey Milk and Other Stories (Firebrand
Books, Ithaca, NY, forthcoming 1988

HerBooks Titles
P.O. Box 7467 • Santa Cruz, CA • 95061

Mail orders welcome. Please include
$.80 postage for the first book, $.25 for each
additional book. Bookstores 40% discount.

Love Me Like You Mean It
poems by
Lesléa Newman
$6.00

To Live With the Weeds
poems by
D.A. Clarke
$7.00

The World Between
Women
an anthology
$7.95

Remember the Fire
Lesbian Sado-masochism
in a post Nazi
Holocaust World
an essay by
Irene Reti
$2.50

Lesbian Words
A Santa Cruz Anthology
$4.95

The Lesbian in Front of
the Classroom
writings by Lesbian
Teachers
$6.50

Between the Lines
an anthology by
Pacific/Asian Lesbians
of Santa Cruz, California
Editors:
C. Chung, A. Kim
A.K. Lemeshewsky
$5.00

Love, Politics and Rescue
in Lesbian Relationships
an essay by
Diana Rabenold
$3.50

Nauseous in Paradise
poems and photographs
Abby Bee
$6.95

HerBooks is now accepting manuscripts for the **Lesbian-Feminist Essay Series**. We are looking for original, personal, passionate and persuasive essays by and about lesbians intended to inspire dialogue among lesbians. Writing should be non-scholarly, non-rhetorical, and accessible; essays which combine poetry and narrative with research are welcome. A few possible topics: how can thin lesbians be allies of fat lesbians, lesbians and co-dependency, sexuality, international lesbianism, lesbian teachers, lesbian ethics and politics . . . Proposals are welcome. Manuscripts should be no longer than 40 typed pages. Send SASE.